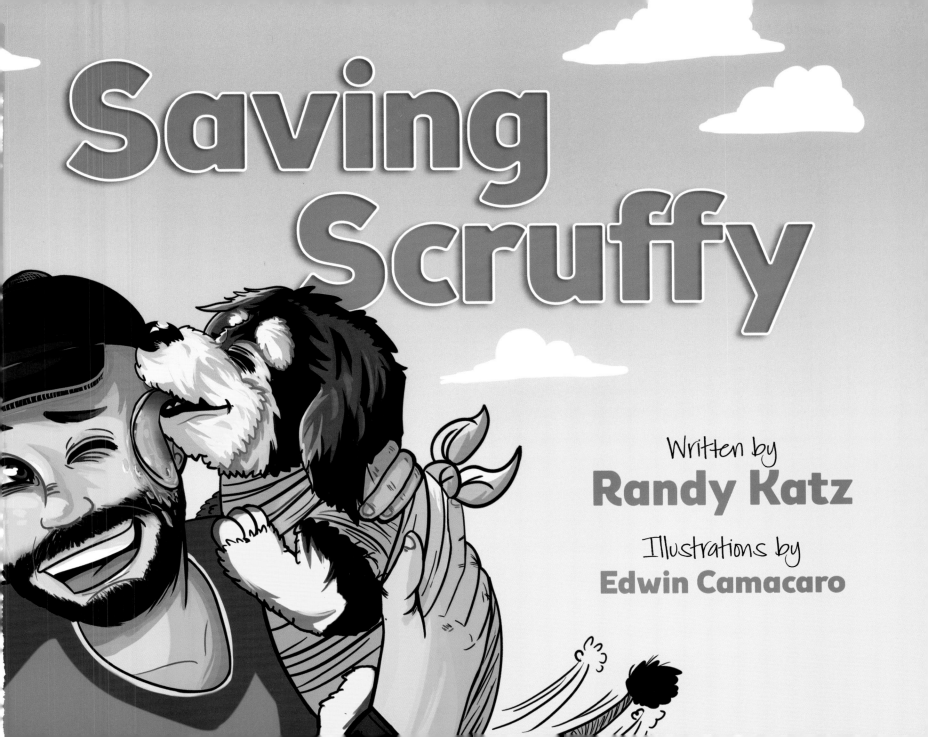

Saving Scruffy

Written by
Randy Katz

Illustrations by
Edwin Camacaro

Saving Scruffy

Text by Randy Katz

Illustrations by Edwin Camacaro

Text and illustrations copyright © 2021 Randy Katz

ISBN: 978-1-7356638-0-7 (print)
ISBN: 978-1-7356638-1-4 (eBook)

LCCN: 2020916312

Publisher's Cataloging-In-Publication Data
(Prepared by The Donohue Group, Inc.)

Names: Katz, Randy, 1975- author. | Camacaro, Edwin, illustrator.

Title: Saving Scruffy / written by Randy Katz ; illustrations by Edwin Camacaro.

Description: [Wilton Manors, Florida] : [Randy Katz], [2021] | Interest age level: 003-008. | Summary: "This is a ... story of a badly hurt puppy named Scruffy who was left abandoned in a box at a fire station. Scruffy's injuries made him different and special. A kindhearted man adopts Scruffy and provides him with a forever home, giving the puppy a second chance. In turn, Scruffy learns that everyone deserves a loving home"--Provided by publisher.

Identifiers: ISBN 9781735663807 (print) | ISBN 9781735663814 (ebook)

Subjects: LCSH: Dog adoption--Juvenile fiction. | Puppies--Wounds and injuries--Juvenile fiction. | Individual differences--Juvenile fiction. | Love--Juvenile fiction. | CYAC: Dog adoption--Fiction. | Dogs--Wounds and injuries--Fiction. | Individual differences--Fiction. | Love--Fiction.

Classification: LCC PZ7.1.K3745 Sa 2021 (print) | LCC PZ7.1.K3745 (ebook) | DDC [E]--dc23

Editor: Gail M.Kearns
Art Director: Penelope C. Paine
Cover and Interior Design: Peri Gabriel Design
Book Production Coordinated by To Press & Beyond

www.savingscruffy.com

Printed in USA

For my best and very brave friend Scruffy,
different and special in every way;
and with thanks to firefighters and animal rescue
programs everywhere.

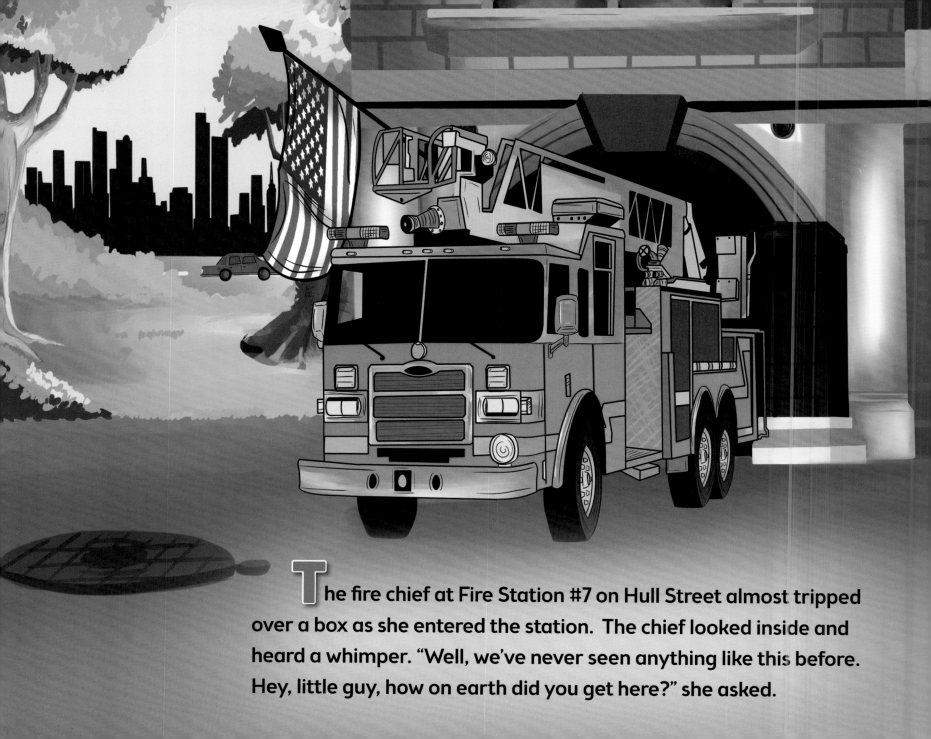

The fire chief at Fire Station #7 on Hull Street almost tripped over a box as she entered the station. The chief looked inside and heard a whimper. "Well, we've never seen anything like this before. Hey, little guy, how on earth did you get here?" she asked.

"Quick, come look," the chief called to the other firefighters. "It's a puppy. Somebody must have left him during the night." She picked up the box and carefully looked under the soft blue blanket he was wrapped in.

There was no note in the box, but the chief could see that the little dog had been badly hurt. His fur was messy, his skin was scraped, and his paws were dirty.

O ther firefighters began to gather around.

"Poor little buddy," one of the firefighters said. "He's certainly looking a bit scruffy."

"That's a good name for him," another firefighter piped up, and, because they didn't know the puppy's name, they called him Scruffy—well, sometimes they called him Mr. Scruffy.

"**W**e'd better get him to a veterinarian right away," the chief said.

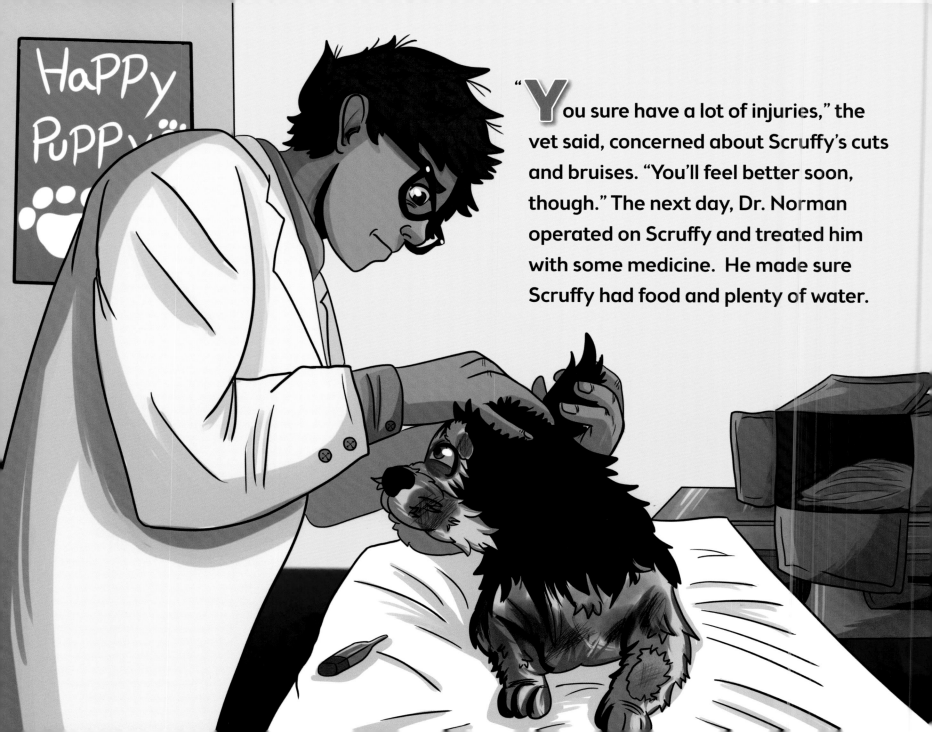

"You sure have a lot of injuries," the vet said, concerned about Scruffy's cuts and bruises. "You'll feel better soon, though." The next day, Dr. Norman operated on Scruffy and treated him with some medicine. He made sure Scruffy had food and plenty of water.

When the fire chief
saw Scruffy again, he was
covered from head to tail with
bandages; but at least he could
still wiggle one ear!

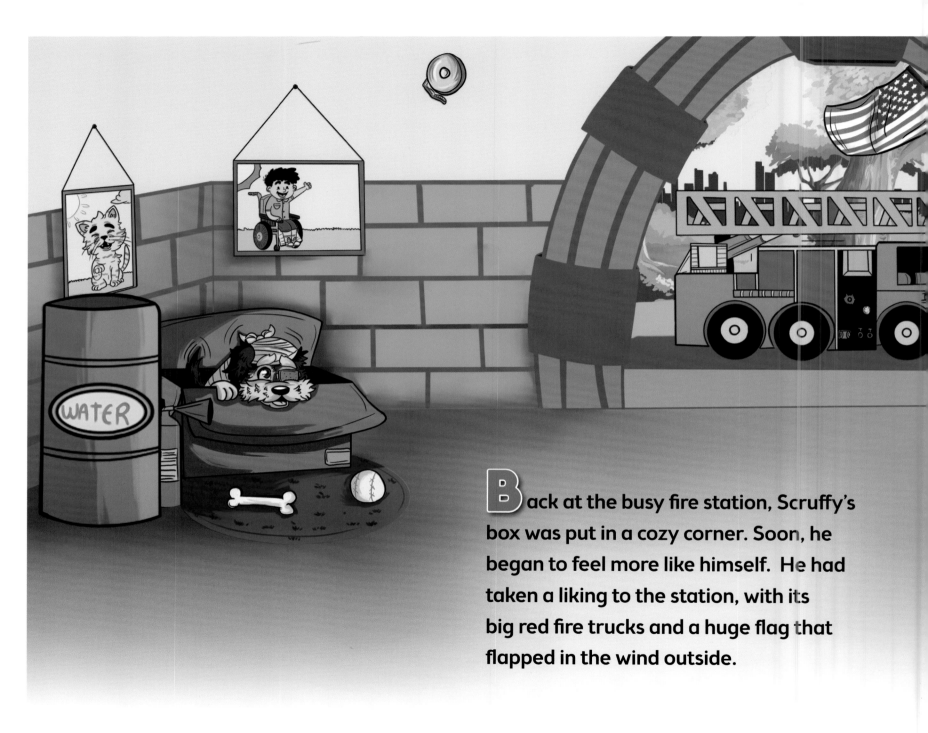

ack at the busy fire station, Scruffy's box was put in a cozy corner. Soon, he began to feel more like himself. He had taken a liking to the station, with its big red fire trucks and a huge flag that flapped in the wind outside.

One of the firefighters helped Mr. Scruffy stand up straight and gave him special treats. Even though they all loved Scruffy, they knew he needed a real home.

When the fire alarm went off and bells started to ring, Scruffy could hardly stand the noise. "Back soon, Scruffy," the firefighters called out as they raced around and jumped into the big red fire trucks.

One sunny afternoon, the fire chief came into the station with a television reporter.

"**W**e usually rescue cats," the chief said, scratching Scruffy behind his ear. "This sweet little dog is a first for us. As soon as his bandages are off, he'll be in fine shape, except for a few scars, and his tail may not wag the same."

Scruffy enjoyed all the attention. He tried to smile and wag his tail as best he could, but he still had so many bandages, his tail hardly moved. The reporter asked the TV viewers if anyone could help Scruffy find a home.

People everywhere saw the news story. Mr. Scruffy became a television and internet star, but he was worried that no one would want him because his scars made him look different, still a bit scruffy, and not like other dogs.

6 NEWS   Puppy Rescued. Looking for a New Home.

cross town, a kindhearted man named Randy watched the broadcast. He could see that Scruffy was a one-of-a-kind dog and that Scruffy's scars made him special. He called the fire station and spoke to one of the firefighters. "I want to be Scruffy's dad," he said. "I will give him a good home."

Randy couldn't get to the fire station fast enough. He grabbed his backpack and was out the door in a flash. His heart was thumping when he met the fire chief and another firefighter.

The fire chief took Randy over to meet Scruffy. "Here he is, he's much better now."

"Hello, Mr. Scruffy," Randy said, bending down to gently stroke the puppy's ear. Scruffy stirred and looked up at Randy. Scruffy was a bit scared, but Randy reached into his backpack and pulled out a red ball that squeaked.

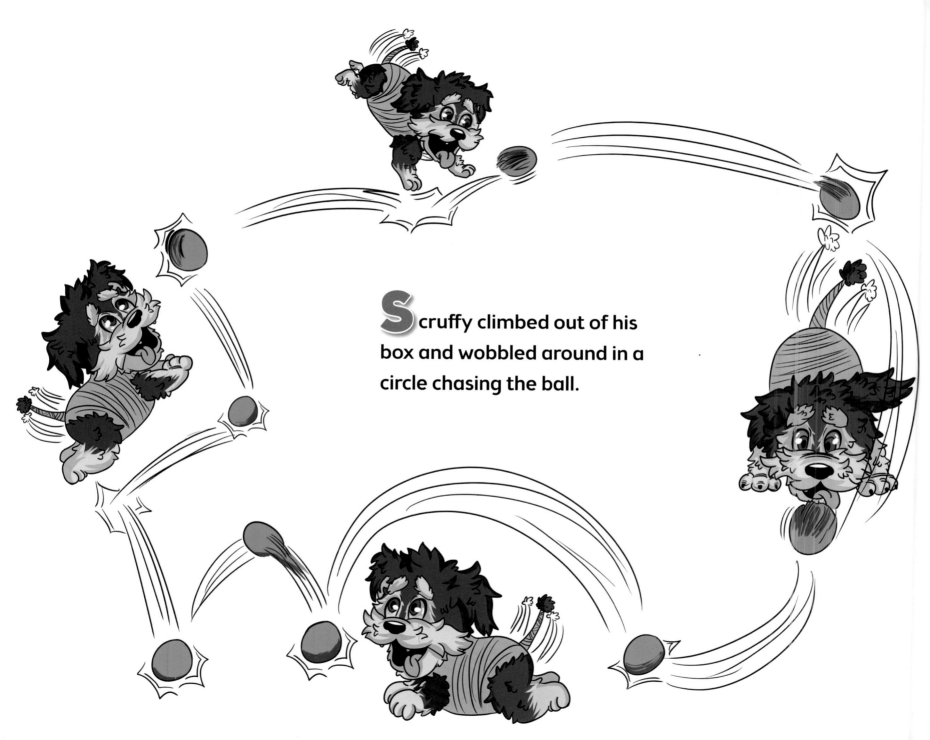

Scruffy climbed out of his box and wobbled around in a circle chasing the ball.

"Go Scruffy!" Randy laughed as he held out his hand. Scruffy barked and gave him his paw for a high-five.

"I'd really like to adopt Scruffy," Randy told the fire chief, picking up Scruffy in his arms. Scruffy felt very safe, and he licked kisses all over Randy's face.

"That's great!" the chief said. The firefighters cheered and clapped. They were happy Scruffy found a new home.

The firefighters put Scruffy up front in one of the big fire trucks. The driver tooted the horn and blasted the siren a couple of times, which got Scruffy really excited.

Randy's house had a big yard, a wooden gate, and a flag outside, just like the fire station. Scruffy felt at home right away.

In a quiet corner of the kitchen there was a soft dog bed with his name on it!

Scruffy got lots of good sniffs on walks with Randy in the neighborhood.

Randy took Scruffy to the coffee shop, and they shared treats.

And they went swimming in the lake so Scruffy could practice his doggy-paddle.

Scruffy loved rolling on the grass in the big yard.

But, most of all, Scruffy loved riding in Randy's car and feeling the fresh air blowing on his face.

Scruffy felt special with his new Dad, and he found out that even if you are different, you can still be loved.

And he was.

Scruffy

Acknowledgments

There are many people to thank for this book, especially Scruffy, who is a daily inspiration in resilience and kindness. A special thank you to the firefighters at the Pompano Beach Fire Department who rescued Scruffy and the team at NBC 6 for helping to raise money for his treatment. I would also like to thank the Fegenbush-Eldredge family, Shane Faullin, Daniel Gibson, Jeana Konstanakopolous, Colin Wright, the Barbour-Ladak family, Henry Chavez, Jack Spence, Marc Levinson, Barbara Martinez, Trinidad Peraza, Tracy Dalton, Rabbi Gil Steinlauf, my parents, and Auntie Nancy, who have always supported me. It remains my hope that Scruffy and his positive, uplifting, and unique story inspires children and adults everywhere to live their lives to the fullest and to embrace the joy that life brings through adversity and love.

About the Author

Randy Katz resides in Florida. Randy is an advocate for adopting dogs. He believes that there are so many precious dogs, like Scruffy, who need love and loving homes. In his spare time, Randy enjoys traveling, CrossFit, adventures, coffee shops, and spending time with his friends, family, and, of course, Scruffy, who still gives Randy paw-bumps! Randy wants to empower people around the world with positive messages and share Scruffy's inspirational story.

About the Illustrator

Edwin (Ed) Camacaro is a cartoonist and illustrator and can be reached on Instagram @sr_ed.

About Scruffy

This is a true story. Scruffy was burned and abandoned at a fire station. Firefighters rescued him. His story was featured on television, and people from all over the world donated money for his surgery. Randy met Scruffy and instantly fell in love. Visit www.savingscruffy.com and follow him on Instagram at @saving.scruffy for more information on Scruffy and his loveable adventures!